MW00927854

Workbook

For

The Tears That Taught Me

(An Implementation Guide to Morgan Richard Olivier's Book)

Greene Press

Copyright © [2024] by [Greene Press]
All rights reserved. No part of this workbook may be reproduced, distributed, or transmitted in any form or by any means, including photocopying, recording, or other electronic or mechanical methods, without the prior written permission of the copyright holder, except for brief quotations embodied in critical reviews and certain other noncommercial uses permitted by copyright law.

This workbook is designed as a companion to the original book and is intended solely for the purpose of enhancing your understanding of the concepts presented in the original book. It is not meant to replace the original book. Please refer to the original book for a complete and in-depth understanding of the subject matter.

Table of Contents

How to Use This Book

Welcome to the companion workbook for The Tears That Taught Me. This workbook is designed to be your personal guide and resource as you explore the key concepts and insights from the original book.

1. Begin with the General Summary: Start your journey by reading the general summary of the original book. This will provide you with an overview of the book's main themes and ideas, helping you establish a solid foundation for the chapters to come.

Exploring Each Chapter

2. Core Lessons: You'll find a section highlighting the key lessons and insights from that particular chapter. Take your time to reflect on these key lessons, as they serve as the foundation for the self-reflection questions that follow.

3. Self-Reflection Questions: Engage actively with the content by answering the self-reflection questions provided at the end of each chapter. These questions are designed to encourage deeper thought and introspection, helping you apply the book's principles to your own life.

Final Self-Evaluation

4. Final Self-Evaluation Questions: As you progress through the workbook, you'll accumulate insights and knowledge. To wrap up your journey, turn to the "Final Self-Evaluation Questions" section at the end of the workbook. These questions encourage you to reflect on your overall understanding and the personal impact of the book's teachings on your life.

Note Section

6. Once you are through with the workbook, use the Personal Notes section to record your thoughts, reflections, and insights. This section is for your own personal use, and can be a

valuable tool for tracking your progress and growth over time.

Note: This workbook is not intended to replace the original book. It is a tool to enhance your understanding and help you integrate the book's wisdom into your daily life. We encourage you to take your time, reflect, and apply the lessons you discover as you progress through this workbook. Your personal growth and development are the ultimate goals, and we hope this companion workbook serves as a valuable resource on your journey.

General Summary

"The Tears That Taught Me" by Morgan Richard Olivier is a compelling collection of poetry and prose that delves deep into the human experience of pain, growth, and resilience. Through unapologetically honest reflections and raw emotions, Olivier invites readers on a journey of self-discovery and healing.

At its core, the book explores the transformative power of tears—the tears shed in moments of anguish, despair, and heartache. Rather than viewing tears as a sign of weakness, Olivier celebrates them as poignant reminders of our capacity to feel and to heal. Each poem and prose piece serves as a testament to the strength that emerges from vulnerability, and the wisdom that arises from suffering.

Throughout the collection, Olivier weaves together themes of courage, forgiveness, and self-acceptance. Readers are encouraged to confront their deepest fears, embrace their flaws and imperfections, and find solace in the knowledge that pain is not without purpose. By embracing the full spectrum of human emotion, from sorrow to joy, readers are invited to embark on a journey of self-discovery and personal growth.

Moreover, "The Tears That Taught Me" is not merely a collection of words on a page; it is a profound exploration of the human condition. Olivier's writing is both lyrical and evocative, drawing readers in with its raw authenticity and emotional depth. Whether grappling with themes of love, loss, or redemption, each poem leaves an indelible mark on the heart and soul of the reader.

Ultimately, "The Tears That Taught Me" demonstrates the tenacity of the human spirit. It is a reminder that even in our darkest moments, there is beauty to be found, and lessons to be learned. Through Olivier's poignant storytelling and profound insights, readers are invited to embrace their own tears as teachers, guiding them towards greater understanding, compassion, and self-discovery.

The Roots

Chapter Summary

In "The Roots," Morgan Richard Olivier delves into the foundational aspects of our lives, symbolized by the roots that anchor us. The poem explores the idea that our past experiences, like roots, shape our present reality. It encourages readers to confront and understand the struggles, trials, and emotional entanglements that have defined them. Through unapologetic reflections, Olivier urges individuals to acknowledge the importance of these roots, not just in terms of hardships but also as sources of strength and resilience. By addressing the roots of our existence, the chapter sets the stage for a journey of self-discovery, acceptance, and personal growth.

Core Lessons

1. Embrace Your Roots: Acknowledge and accept the entirety of your past, recognizing that both challenges and triumphs have contributed to your present self.

2. Learn from Pain: Understand that even the most difficult experiences carry valuable lessons, fostering growth, empathy, and strength.

3. Forgiveness Leads to Freedom: Encourage forgiveness, whether directed towards others or oneself, as a crucial step toward letting go of the weight of the past.

4. Speak Your Truth: Embrace the power of authenticity and sharing your experiences, recognizing the impact your story can have on your life and the lives of others.

5. Find Beauty in Burdens: Discover the transformative beauty that can emerge from hardships, viewing them not as setbacks but as opportunities for personal evolution.

Introspection Questions

1. What aspects of your past do you find challenging to confront, and why?

_____

_____

_____

_____

_____

_____

2. In what ways have your past struggles contributed to your current strengths and resilience?

_____

3. How do you typically deal with pain and difficult emotions?

_____

_____

4. Are there areas in your life where forgiveness could bring about a sense of freedom?

_____

_____

_____

_____

_____

_____

5. How comfortable are you with speaking your truth and sharing your authentic experiences?

_____

_____

_____

_____

_____

_____

6. What wisdom have you gained from your past burdens that can guide your present actions?

_____

_____

_____

_____

_____

_____

_____

7. Do you tend to focus more on the negative or positive aspects of your past experiences?

_____

_____

_____

_____

_____

_____

_____

8. In what ways can you reframe your perspective to find beauty in the challenges you've faced?

_____

_____

_____

_____

_____

_____

Action Plan

1. Roots Visualization: Close your eyes, visualize your life as a tree with roots extending into the past. Explore each root, reflecting on significant moments and emotions associated with them.

2. Letter of Forgiveness: Write a letter forgiving either yourself or someone else for past grievances. Allow yourself to release the emotional burden and experience the freedom forgiveness brings.

3. Authentic Storytelling: Share a personal experience authentically with someone you trust. Notice the impact of vulnerability on your connection and understanding of each other's lives.

Pruning To Peace

Chapter Summary

In "Pruning To Peace," Morgan Richard Olivier guides readers through the metaphorical process of pruning, emphasizing the transformative power of letting go and making peace with the past. The chapter explores the idea that, much like a skilled gardener prunes away dead or overgrown branches to allow new growth, individuals must also trim away the negativity and pain in their lives. Olivier encourages readers to acknowledge the necessity of shedding what no longer serves them, fostering an environment conducive to personal growth. The central theme revolves around embracing the cathartic release of pruning, allowing for a more peaceful and flourishing existence.

Core Lessons

1. Letting Go Leads to Growth: The chapter emphasizes that releasing the weight of past burdens is essential for personal growth. Just as pruning promotes new life in a garden, letting go of emotional baggage allows individuals to flourish.

2. Acceptance of Impermanence: Readers learn that life, like a garden, is ever-changing. Accepting this impermanence and being open to the ebb and flow of experiences fosters resilience and adaptability.

3. Self-Reflection as a Pruning Tool: Encouraging readers to engage in self-reflection, the chapter highlights its role as a tool for personal pruning. Understanding oneself allows for intentional removal of negativity and promotes self-discovery.

4. The Healing Power of Release: Olivier explores the concept that releasing pain and emotional baggage can be a healing process,

allowing individuals to find peace within themselves.

5. Resilience Through Renewal: The chapter underscores the idea that just as pruned plants renew and thrive, individuals can cultivate resilience by renewing their perspectives and attitudes.

Introspection Questions

1. How does holding onto past pain hinder your personal growth?

_____

_____

_____

_____

_____

2. In what areas of your life do you need to prune and let go?

3. What emotions or memories do you find challenging to release?

_____

_____

_____

_____

_____

_____

4. How does self-reflection contribute to the pruning of negative influences in your life?

_____

_____

_____

_____

_____

_____

_____

5. Can you identify patterns or habits that need pruning for a more peaceful existence?

_____

_____

_____

_____

_____

_____

_____

6. What aspects of your life could benefit from a
fresh perspective and renewal?

_____

_____

_____

_____

_____

_____

7. In what ways does acceptance of impermanence contribute to emotional well-being?

_____

_____

_____

_____

_____

_____

8. How can the act of releasing emotional burdens contribute to your overall sense of peace?

_____

_____

_____

_____

_____

_____

_____

Action Plan

1. Emotional Inventory: Create a list of emotions tied to past experiences. Reflect on each emotion's impact on your present well-being and consider ways to release or transform them.

2. Symbolic Pruning: Use a visual representation, like drawing or crafting, to symbolize aspects of your life that need pruning. Reflect on the symbolism and let it guide your journey toward peace.

3. Letter of Release: Write a letter to yourself or others involved in past pain. Express your emotions and release them through written words. Consider whether you want to share the letter or keep it for personal catharsis.

Bloom Boldly

Chapter Summary

In "Bloom Boldly," Morgan Richard Olivier encourages readers to courageously embrace the process of growth and transformation. The chapter delves into the concept of boldness as an essential element in navigating life's challenges and opportunities. Through poetic reflections and prose, Olivier illustrates how embracing boldness allows individuals to confront their fears, uncertainties, and limitations, ultimately leading to personal empowerment and self-discovery. By blooming boldly, readers are inspired to step outside their comfort zones, pursue their passions, and embrace the full spectrum of their potential.

This chapter celebrates the resilience and tenacity required to bloom boldly in the face of adversity. Olivier reminds readers that growth often occurs in the most unexpected places and situations. Through vulnerability and authenticity, individuals can cultivate inner strength and resilience, transcending limitations and societal expectations. "Bloom Boldly" serves as a poignant reminder that true growth and transformation arise from the willingness to embrace discomfort, take risks, and trust in the inherent beauty of one's journey.

Core Lessons

1. Embrace Fear: Recognize that fear is a natural part of the growth process. Instead of allowing fear to hinder progress, use it as fuel to propel yourself forward.

2. Cultivate Courage: Boldness is not the absence of fear but the willingness to act despite it. Cultivate courage by taking small steps outside your comfort zone each day.

3. Embrace Vulnerability: Authentic growth requires vulnerability. Allow yourself to be seen and heard, even in moments of uncertainty and discomfort.

4. Trust the Process: Transformation takes time and patience. Trust in the journey, knowing that every experience, whether positive or negative, contributes to your growth.

5. Celebrate Progress: Acknowledge and celebrate your accomplishments, no matter how small. Each stride forward demonstrates your strength and resilience.

Introspection Questions

1. What does "blooming boldly" mean to you personally?

_____

_____

_____

_____

_____

_____

_____

2. In what areas of your life do you feel the most
fear or resistance?

_____

_____

_____

_____

_____

_____

3. How have past experiences shaped your willingness to take risks?

_____

_____

_____

_____

_____

_____

4. What steps can you take to cultivate courage in your daily life?

_____

_____

_____

_____

_____

_____

_____

5. How comfortable are you with being vulnerable? Why?

_____

_____

_____

_____

_____

6. What do you fear most about embracing discomfort and uncertainty?

7. Do you trust in the inherent beauty of your journey? Why or why not?

_____

_____

_____

_____

_____

_____

8. How can you celebrate your progress, no matter how small?

_____

_____

_____

_____

_____

_____

_____

Action Plan

1. Courage Journal: Keep a journal where you document moments of courage, no matter how small. Reflect on how each act of bravery contributes to your personal growth.

2. Fear Inventory: Make a list of your fears and the reasons behind them. Challenge yourself to confront one fear each week, starting with the least intimidating.

3. Bold Action Plan: Identify one bold action you've been hesitant to take. Break it down into smaller, manageable steps, and create a timeline for execution. Take the first step today.

Final Self Assessment Questions

1. How has "The Tears That Taught Me" influenced your understanding of personal growth?

_____

_____

_____

_____

_____

_____

2. Which specific poems or prose passages resonated with you the most, and why?

_____

_____

_____

_____

_____

_____

3. Can you describe any changes in your mindset or behavior since engaging with the book?

_____

_____

_____

_____

_____

_____

_____

4. In what ways have you applied the principles of courage and vulnerability discussed in the book to your own life?

_____

_____

_____

_____

_____

_____

_____

5. Reflect on a moment when you felt particularly moved or inspired by the book. What did you learn from this experience?

_____

_____

_____

_____

_____

_____

_____

6. How do you plan to incorporate the lessons of self-acceptance and resilience into your daily life?

_____

_____

_____

_____

_____

_____

7. Describe a situation where you were able to overcome a challenge using insights gained from the book.

_____

_____

_____

_____

_____

_____

_____

8. Have you noticed any shifts in your perspective on forgiveness or empathy as a result of reading "The Tears That Taught Me"?

_____

_____

_____

_____

_____

_____

_____

9. What recurring themes or motifs in the book do you identify with most strongly, and why?

_____

_____

_____

_____

_____

_____

_____

10. How do you envision your continued growth and development, and how will the book support you on this journey?

_____

_____

_____

_____

_____

_____

11. Reflect on a moment of triumph or resilience in your life. How does it align with the themes explored in the book?

_____

_____

_____

_____

_____

_____

_____

12. Can you identify any specific actions or changes you've made in your life after reading "The Tears That Taught Me"?

_____

_____

_____

_____

---

13. Describe the impact of the book on your relationship with pain and adversity.

---

14. How has your understanding of truth and authenticity evolved through engaging with the book?

_____

_____

_____

_____

_____

_____

15. Looking back, what do you believe is the greatest benefit you've gained from reading "The Tears That Taught Me"?

_____

_____

_____

_____

_____

_____

Personal Notes

Made in the USA
Las Vegas, NV
06 May 2024

89518601R00036